D0265018

Country File
South Africa

Ian Graham

W
FRANKLIN WATTS
LONDON • SYDNEY

MORAY COUNCIL LIBRARIES & INFO.SERVICES

2O 13 72 43		
Askews		
J968.066		

First published in 2004 by
Franklin Watts
96 Leonard Street, London
EC2A 4XD

Franklin Watts Australia
45–51 Huntley Street,
Alexandria, NSW 2015

© 2004 Bender Richardson White
All rights reserved
No part of this publication may be reproduced, stored in a retrieval system, or transmitted in any form or by any means electronic, mechanical, photocopying, recording or otherwise without the prior written permission of the copyright owner.

COUNTRY FILE: SOUTH AFRICA produced for Franklin Watts by Bender Richardson White, PO Box 266, Uxbridge, UK.
Editor: Lionel Bender
Designer and Page Make-up: Ben White
Picture Researcher: Cathy Stastny
Cover Make-up: Mike Pilley, Radius
Production: Kim Richardson

Graphics and Maps: Stefan Chabluk

Consultant: Dr Terry Jennings, a former teacher and university lecturer. He is now a full-time writer of children's geography and science books.

A CIP catalogue record for this book is available from the British Library.

ISBN 0-7496-5380-9

Manufactured in China

Picture Credits

Pages 1: South African Tourism. 3: Corbis Images Inc.. 5: Eye Ubiquitous/Peter Kingsford. 7: Robert Harding/Fraser Hall. 9: Eye Ubiquitous/Gallo Images. 10, 11, 12 top: South African Tourism. 12 bottom: Corbis Images/M. L. Sinibaldi. 15: Robert Harding/C. Jopp. 17: Robert Harding. 18, 19, 20, 21, 22: South African Tourism. 23: Eye Ubiquitous/Gallo Images. 24: Robert Harding/Robert Cundy. 25: Paul Reeves. 26: Corbis Images/Peter Tumley. 27: Robert Harding/Fraser Hall. 28: Eye Ubiquitous/Liz Gordon. 30, 31: South African Tourism.

Cover Photo: Corbis Images Inc./Mark A. Johnson

The Author

Ian Graham is a full-time writer and editor of non-fiction books. He has written more than 100 books for children.

Note to parents and teachers

Every effort has been made by the Publishers to ensure that the websites in this book are suitable for children, that they are of the highest educational value, and that they contain no inappropriate or offensive material. However, because of the nature of the Internet, it is impossible to guarantee that the contents of these sites will not be altered. We strongly advise that Internet access is supervised by a responsible adult.

Contents

Welcome to South Africa

The Republic of South Africa (RSA), known simply as South Africa, occupies most of the southern tip of Africa. Two great oceans, the Atlantic and Indian Oceans, meet off its southern shores.

South Africa is about the same size as France and Spain combined, or just under twice the size of the US state of Texas. It measures roughly 1,400 kilometres from north to south and 1,600 kilometres from east to west. In addition to the land on the African continent, South Africa includes Prince Edward Islands (Marion Island and Prince Edward Island), located about 2,000 kilometres south-east of the mainland in the southern Indian Ocean.

South Africa is known for its magnificent game reserves, national parks, unspoilt coastline and its world-class athletes and sports teams, such as the Springboks rugby team. It is also famous for its success in overcoming its troubled past without the wars that have torn other African nations apart.

DATABASE

Regions and neighbours

South Africa has three capital cities (see page 30) and is divided into nine provinces. Most of the people live in the eastern and southern provinces. South Africa shares borders with Botswana, Lesotho, Mozambique, Namibia, Swaziland and Zimbabwe. Lesotho is a 'land-locked' country, completely surrounded by South Africa. Swaziland is also almost completely surrounded by South Africa.

Government buildings, dating from European colonial times, and modern office buildings fill the centre of Durban, the capital of Kwazulu-Natal Province and South Africa's second-largest city. ▼

4

20°E   24°E   28°E   32°E

20°S

ZIMBABWE

NAMIBIA

BOTSWANA

Tropic of Capricorn

Messina

Limpopo

Louis Trichardt

Pietersburg

24°S

KALAHARI

D E S E R T

**M
O
Z
A
M
B
I
Q
U
E**

Sun City

Molopo

Mafikeng

H I G H V E L D

Krugersdorp

PRETORIA

Johannesburg

Vereeniging

Vaal

SWAZILAND

Vryburg

Kuruman

Vaaldam

Welkom

28°S

Upington

Orange

Kimberley

Champagne
Castle

Ladysmith

Empangeni

Kenhardt

Douglas

BLOEMFONTEIN

Pietermaritzburg

Springbok

S O U T H

LESOTHO

Durban

A F R I C A

Port Shepstone

Carnarvon

Burgersdorp

Port St. Johns

Calvinia

Victoria West

Bamboesberge

Clanwilliam

Gt Fish

32°S

Saldanha

Beaufort West

I N D I A N

G R E A T   K A R O O

East London

Malmesbury

Kirkwood

CAPE TOWN

Grahamstown

Table Mountain

Port Elizabeth

O C E A N

*Cape of Good
Hope*

Hermanus

Mosselbaai
(Mossel Bay)

S O U T H

A T L A N T I C

	Mountains	△ Mountain peak
	Grassland and farming	
□	Capitals	○ Major city
—	Country boundary	

O C E A N

0   400 Miles

0   400 Kilometres

The Land

M ost of South Africa consists of a high, arid plateau ringed by desert, hills, mountains and a low-lying coastal region.

The plateau rises from a height of about 600 metres in the west to 2,440 metres in the east. The central part of the plateau is called the *Highveld* (an Afrikaans word meaning 'high grassland'). The Kalahari Desert lies to the north. The mountains and steep slopes that separate the Highveld from the lower surrounding ground are called the Great Escarpment.

Enormous forces in the Earth's crust have pushed up a series of mountain ranges in the south-west of the country. They contain one of the world's most famous mountains, the flat-topped Table Mountain that overlooks Cape Town.

Animals

South Africa's varied landscape supports a wide variety of plant and animal life. It is home to all three of the biggest land mammals (elephant, rhinoceros and hippopotamus), the tallest (giraffe), the fastest (cheetah) and also the smallest (the pygmy shrew). More than 20,000 different species of plants – one-tenth of all the plants on Earth – grow in South Africa.

Mammals include: Aardvark, baboon, buffalo, bat-eared fox, bushbaby, bushbuck, Cape fox, cheetah, civet, colobus monkey, eland, elephant, fruit bat, giraffe, hartebeest, hippopotamus, honey badger, hyena, impala, jackal, kudu, leopard, lion, mongoose, mouse, nyala, otter, pangolin, porcupine, pygmy shrew, reedbuck, rhinoceros, rat, rock rabbit, sable, samango monkey, serval, spotted cat, springbok, tree squirrel, vervet monkey, warthog, waterbuck, wildebeest and zebra.

Rainfall

South Africa's rainfall is concentrated in the eastern half of the country and on the southern coast.

Plants

Among South Africa's flora are such exotic trees as stinkwoods, ironwoods, baobabs, acacias and eucalyptuses.

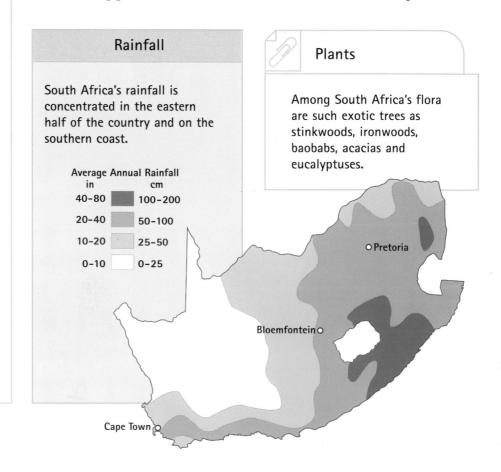

Average Annual Rainfall

in		cm
40–80		100–200
20–40		50–100
10–20		25–50
0–10		0–25

Pretoria

Bloemfontein

Cape Town

Climate

South Africa's climate is generally warm and dry. The east and west coasts enjoy very different weather because of the ocean currents that flow past them. The cold Benguela Current flows northwards, cooling the west coast and reducing rainfall there. On the other side of the country, the warm Mozambique and Agulhas Currents flow south. They warm the air, which picks up moisture from the sea and blows inland. As it cools, it sheds the water as rain.

Rainfall on the east coast of the country can be more than 100 centimetres a year, while parts of the west coast receive less than 5 centimetres. Summer in South Africa lasts from November to March and winter is between May and September. During winter, cold air from the south polar region moves northwards and cools the south coast.

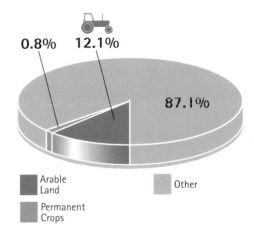

0.8%   12.1%

87.1%

Arable Land   Other

Permanent Crops

▲ Land use in South Africa. More than three-quarters of the land is mountain, desert, urban areas and uncultivated land (defined as 'Other').

Cape Town's annual rainfall of about 61cm reaches a peak in June. The city and surroundings on the west coast experience many cloudless, hot summer days and mild, wet winter days. ►►

The Mediterranean-type climate of the Hottentot's Holland Mountains region east of Cape Town is ideal for growing fruit including grapes. Vineyards cover the mountain slopes. The nearby town of Stellenbosch is a major wine-producing centre. ▼

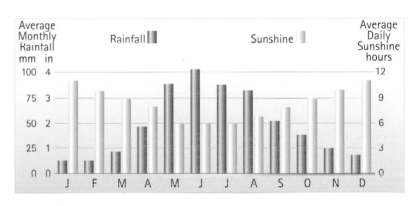

Average Monthly Rainfall mm in

Rainfall   Sunshine

Average Daily Sunshine hours

J F M A M J J A S O N D

Birds, Reptiles and Amphibians

South African birds include: Crane, green twinspot, hoopoe, kingfisher, martial eagle, ostrich, jackass penguin, robin, sunbird.

Reptiles and amphibians include species of: Crocodile, frog, puff adder, berg adder, terrapin, toad, tortoise.

7

The People

The population of South Africa is such a diverse mixture of different groups of people from all over the continent and other parts of the world that the country has been nicknamed the 'rainbow nation'.

Each group has its own culture, traditions, cuisine, history and language. Because of South Africa's past, when individuals were separated according to their racial background, people were often described according to their colour or where they came from. These descriptions have survived to the present-day.

Of the total population of about 44 million, 77 per cent (34 million) are black Africans. They belong to four main groups – Nguni, Sotho, Shangaan-Tsonga and Venda. Each group is further divided into smaller subgroups. The Zulu and Xhosa are the two biggest sub-groups of the Nguni.

Language

South Africa has 11 official languages – Afrikaans, English, Ndebele, North Sotho, South Sotho, Swazi, Tsonga, Tswana, Venda, Xhosa and Zulu. Zulu speakers are the most numerous (9 million).

Ancient history

Early ancestors of modern humans, called *Australopithecus* (meaning 'southern ape'), lived in South Africa 3 million years ago. Their remains have been found in Northern Cape Province and the Transvaal region. During the Stone Age, *Australopithecus* was replaced by more advanced creatures called *Homo erectus*, who made stone tools. By 500,000 years ago, they had evolved into our own species, *Homo sapiens*. Their remains have been found in the Western Cape and Mpumalanga. By 200,000 years ago, they had become modern humans.

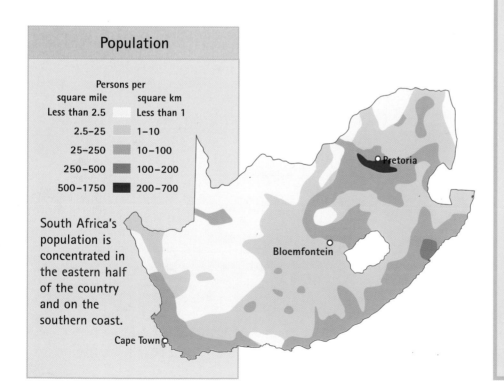

Population

Persons per

square mile	square km
Less than 2.5	Less than 1
2.5–25	1–10
25–250	10–100
250–500	100–200
500–1750	200–700

South Africa's population is concentrated in the eastern half of the country and on the southern coast.

Pretoria

Bloemfontein

Cape Town

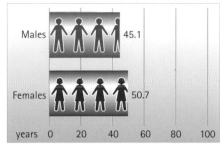

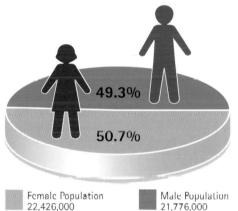

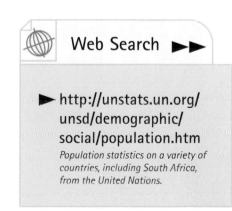

Life expectancy is low and may fall even lower because of the disease HIV/AIDS.

◄◄ Many Zulus live as self-sufficient farmers, as here in Kwazulu-Natal.

Female Population
22,426,000

Male Population
21,776,000

South Africa's population is very evenly balanced, but there are slightly more females than males.

The white population forms 11 per cent (4.8 million) of the total. Almost two-thirds of them are descendants of Dutch and German immigrants. They are called Afrikaners and they speak a language similar to Dutch, called Afrikaans. They live mainly in the Gauteng and Orange Free State Provinces. English-speaking white people live mainly in the Eastern and Western Cape and Kwazulu-Natal.

There are two more population groups. About 3 million people described as 'Coloureds' as their skin colour is a blend of black and white. They are mainly descendants of Dutch immigrants, Africans and slaves. They live mainly in the Northern and Western Cape Provinces. Finally, there are about 1 million Indians, who live mainly in Kwazulu-Natal.

Web Search ►►

► http://unstats.un.org/
unsd/demographic/
social/population.htm
Population statistics on a variety of countries, including South Africa, from the United Nations.

Urban and Rural Life

J ust over half of South Africans live in cities and towns. Urban and rural life in South Africa are at opposite ends of the scale of lifestyles. Its cities are as modern as anywhere in the world, but conditions in its rural areas are still very basic and life is difficult.

Johannesburg, its largest city, is about the same size as New York. There are skyscrapers, cinemas, fast-food restaurants, clubs and modern shops with the latest goods and fashions. The streets are busy with people and traffic. At night, the buildings and streets are brightly lit.

By contrast, in rural areas, many people live in huts built from mud bricks or shacks made from corrugated iron, waste wood or even cardboard. In many cases, there are no gas or electricity supplies and no clean, running water. Usually, water is collected from a shared well or local river.

An increasing number of South Africans are moving from rural areas to large towns and cities. ▼

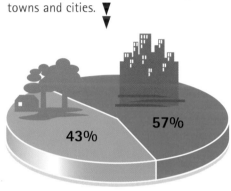

57%

43%

■ Percentage of Population Living in Urban Areas

■ Percentage of Population Living in Rural Areas

Bloemfontein is the capital and largest city in Free State Province. It grew rapidly in the 1960s and 1970s. ▼

Percentage of urban and rural populations with access to sources of clean drinking water. ▼

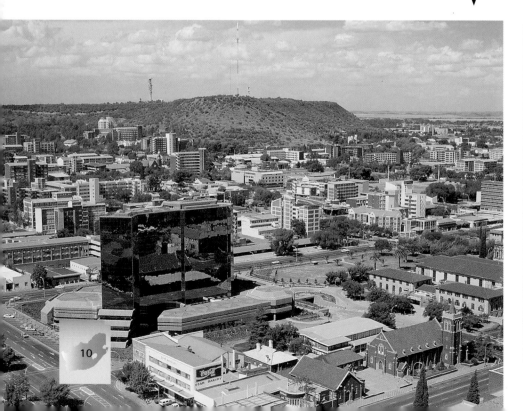

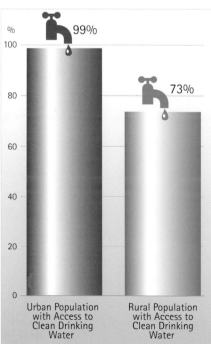

%

100

99%

80

73%

60

40

20

0

Urban Population with Access to Clean Drinking Water

Rural Population with Access to Clean Drinking Water

The Digital Divide

People In South Africa's towns and cities have easy access to modern communications and digital services. Mobile phones, computers and the World Wide Web are all readily available. In many rural areas, there are few telephone lines or computers.

In some parts of the country, telecentres are being set up to offer people computer training and access to telephones and electronic mail. Computer lessons are also given in some schools. Mobile training centres visit schools that have no computers of their own. The Soweto Digital Village was set up in 1997 to serve Soweto and surrounding communities.

Many native black South Africans still live in traditional villages, like this Zulu settlement. ►►

Soweto

The largest black community in South Africa lives in Soweto, a sprawling urban development to the south-west of Johannesburg. It has a population of about 4 million. Its name comes from South-western Townships. Soweto covers more than 100 square kilometres. It stands on land set aside for black people who flocked to the area for work when gold was discovered there in 1886. At first, it was a chaotic collection of slums and shanty-towns. These were replaced with permanent housing from the 1940s onwards.

Web Search ►►

► http://unstats.un.org/ unsd/demographic/ social/hum-set.htm
Urban and rural population statistics for a variety of countries, including South Africa, from the United Nations.

► http://peacecorps.org/ kids/world/africa/ southafrica.html
Stories from teachers and other workers mostly from North America who volunteer to work in less developed parts of the world, including rural South Africa.

Farming and Fishing

▲ On small-scale farms, much of the work is done by hand. These farm workers are harvesting beetroots.

Ports such as Cape Town handle fishing boats, boats carrying farm produce and other goods, and pleasure craft. ▼

Farming in South Africa is made more difficult by a shortage of water in many parts of the country, especially in the western half. Just over one-tenth of the land area can be used for intensive farming using rainfall only. Elsewhere, irrigation is necessary.

Farmers have had to adapt to the weather conditions in different parts of the country. In the driest areas, sheep and goats graze the sparse pasture. In areas with a little more rainfall, cattle can be kept. Dairy herds are kept near the most densely populated areas.

Maize (corn on the cob) and wheat are grown on a large scale – 3.5 million hectares are planted with maize and 860,000 hectares with wheat. Much of this land is irrigated. Irrigation also allows grapes, citrus fruit and vegetables to be grown. Pineapples, bananas and avocados are the most important fruits; tomatoes are also an important crop. About 1 million South Africans work in agriculture.

Viticulture

Viticulture (growing grapes) has been going on at the southern tip of Africa since the seventeenth century. Today, about 100,000 hectares of vineyards produce wine grapes, making South Africa the world's eighth biggest wine producer.

Commercial fishing

South Africa's coastline of almost 3,000 kilometres yields 600,000 tonnes of fish and shellfish a year. Cape hake, anchovies and pilchards are the dominant species. The commercial fishing industry employs about 27,000 people. In addition, about 750,000 people fish for fun and sport. Leisure fishing employs more than 130,000 people. No fishing, whether commercial or for leisure, is allowed without a permit. Fishery control officers enforce the law to protect and conserve the country's valuable marine life.

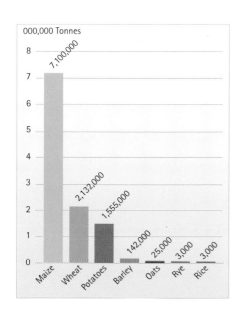

▲ By weight, cereals including maize, wheat, barley and rice, and potatoes are by far the most important crops.

Water management

The Orange River Project is South Africa's biggest water management scheme. Dams on the Orange River – South Africa's longest – provide water for irrigation, hydro-electric power and urban water supplies.

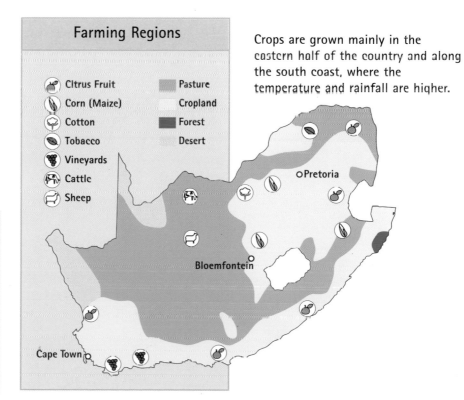

Crops are grown mainly in the eastern half of the country and along the south coast, where the temperature and rainfall are higher.

Resources and Industry

Much of South Africa's wealth comes from the diamonds and gold that were discovered there in the nineteenth century. Their great value transformed South Africa from a mainly agricultural economy to one of the wealthiest and most industrialized nations on the African continent.

Today, South Africa's minerals industry generates almost half of the country's export earnings. In addition to diamonds and gold, valuable metals, such as platinum are mined, too. South Africa is the world's largest producer of both platinum and chromium. It is also the world's third largest exporter of coal and the world's largest producer of liquid fuels and chemicals made from coal. It has more than 60 coal mines, 50 diamond producers and 50 gold producers. Coal is not only exported, it is also used to generate electricity within South Africa itself. Almost all of the country's electricity is produced from coal.

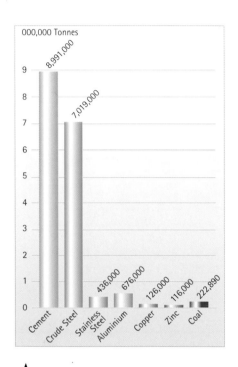

▲ Annual mineral and industrial output by weight.

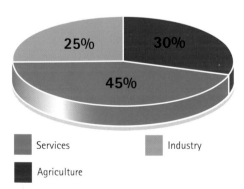

Services
Industry
Agriculture

▲ Only one-quarter of all South Africans work in industry (which includes mining).

Resources and Industry

- Car Manufacture
- Coal
- Iron Ore
- Silver
- Tin
- Copper
- Gold
- Uranium
- Diamonds
- Food Processing
- Textiles
- Hydro-electricity

South Africa's mining operations are concentrated in the north-east of the country.

○ Pretoria

Bloemfontein

Cape Town

▲
▲ Melted raw gold is poured into moulds to make blocks called ingots.

Manufacturing

Earnings from mineral exports allowed manufacturing to grow rapidly during the 1960s. Food processing, textiles, metals and chemicals are particularly important today. The chemical industry developed in part to manufacture the explosives used in the mining industry, but it now produces a wide range of chemicals for all kinds of uses. Other manufactured goods and materials include cars, ships, building materials and electronic equipment.

The tourism industry is an increasingly important contributor to the economy. South Africa is the most popular tourist destination in Africa. Tourism not only generates valuable income, it also employs nearly a million people in airlines, tour operators, car hire companies, coach operators, hotels, restaurants, visitor attractions and other parts of the industry. Many of the tourists are attracted by South Africa's wildlife and vast landscapes, which are therefore protected and conserved as valuable natural resources.

Valuable Resources

South Africa's mines produce about 400 tonnes of raw gold and 2 tonnes of raw diamonds every year. Its factories produce finished metals such as steel, aluminium and copper pipes, cans and sheets.

Web Search ▶▶

▶ http://minerals.usgs.gov/minerals/pubs/country/africa.html#tp
Data on South Africa's mineral deposits provided by the US Geological Survey.

▶ http://minerals.usgs.gov/minerals/pubs/country/maps/92359.gif
A map of South Africa's mineral deposits provided by the US Geological Survey.

Transport

Speed Limits

The speed limit on small rural roads is 80 kph. On main roads outside residential areas, the speed limit is 120 kph. Within towns, speed limits vary from place to place. All vehicles in South Africa drive on the left side of the road, and wearing a seat belt is compulsory.

South Africa has one of the most modern and well-maintained transport systems in Africa. Its major cities are linked by roads, railways and air routes.

For people without their own cars, buses provide the fastest way of getting around. There are three types of buses. The most comfortable, and most expensive, are the spacious, air-conditioned coaches used mainly by tourists and executives. Local people travel more often by smaller 'African buses' and 'minibus taxis'. African buses cost less to use, but they are crowded and less reliable. Minibus taxis are the least expensive but are often dangerously overcrowded and many of them operate illegally.

About 500,000 tonnes of freight are carried by road every year, so there are a lot of lorries on the roads, especially on the intercity highways.

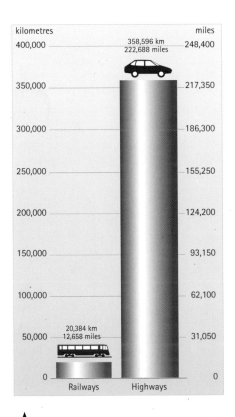

▲ Comparative length of the railway and roadway systems.

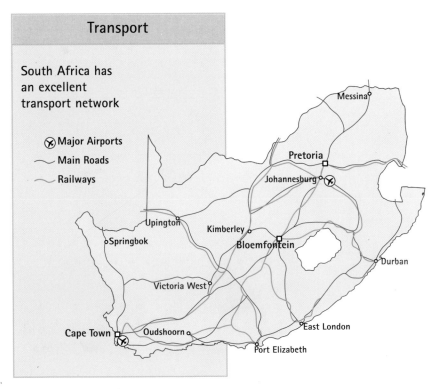

Transport

South Africa has an excellent transport network

- ⊗ Major Airports
- Main Roads
- Railways

Railways

Local and suburban trains serve all the main cities and towns. The biggest cities are linked by long-distance express trains. A luxury express train called the *Blue Train* operates between Cape Town, Port Elizabeth and Pretoria and goes north to Victoria Falls, Zambia. The Trans-Orange service operates between Cape Town and Durban. The Trans-Natal Express links Durban and Johannesburg.

There are steam train services, too, run mainly for tourists. Railways also carry most of the freight traffic within South Africa and to neighbouring countries.

Air and sea

South Africa's harbours are the biggest and best equipped in Africa. The seven largest and most important ports are Cape Town, Durban, East London, Mossel Bay, Saldanha, Port Elizabeth and Richards Bay at Empangeni. Container ships, oil tankers and big cargo ships transport essential supplies, raw materials and manufactured goods between these commercial ports and ports all over the world.

South Africa has excellent air links with the rest of the world. Cities and large towns within South Africa are connected by airways, too. There are daily flights between Cape Town, Johannesburg, Pretoria, Durban, East London, Bloemfontein, Kimberley and Port Elizabeth. Connecting flights link these cities to outlying provincial towns.

▲ Diesel and electric trains carry freight throughout the country.

🌐 **Web Search** ►►

► http://www.transport.gov.za
The South Africa government Department of Transport site.

► http://www.nra.co.za
The National Roads Agency of South Africa provides data on roadways and traffic.

Education

There are about 12 million people of all ages in education in South Africa. Basic education is compulsory and provided free by the state.

Every year, more than a million South African children begin their education at one of the country's 22,000 primary schools. They usually begin school when they are about 7 years old. They attend lessons from Monday to Friday. Primary school lasts from grade 1 to grade 6. Some primary schools also have a pre-school year, called grade 0 or R (reception). At the end of grade 6, children move on to one of the country's 6,000 high schools.

Grades 1 to 9 are compulsory, but attendance in grades 10, 11 and 12 is voluntary. Only about half of the children who start school are still there in grade 12. The rest have left. The government is working to reduce this high drop-out rate so as to increase the overall level of education.

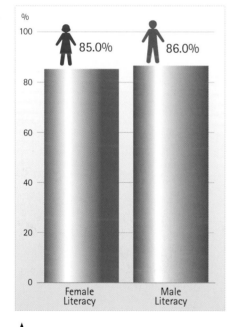

%
100

85.0%   86.0%

80

60

40

20

0

Female
Literacy

Male
Literacy

▲ More than 8 in 10 South African men and women have a basic level of literacy, which is one of the highest levels on the African continent.

Graduate students at a college of higher education. ►►

◄◄ Primary school children are often taken on visits to national museums as part of their education.

49.4%

50.6%

Male/Female Primary School Pupils
Total 8,160,000

Proportions of girls and boys in primary education.

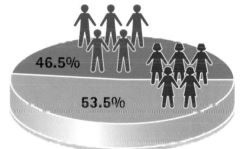

46.5%

53.5%

Male/Female Secondary School Pupils
Total 3,570,000

Proportions of boys and girls in secondary education.

Higher education

To enter one of South Africa's 21 universities, students must pass examinations in a minimum of three subjects at a sufficiently high grade. In addition to universities, 15 technikons (technical colleges) provide technology-related courses to degree level. More than a million students attend a university, technikon or another type of college.

The legacy of the past

Up to 1994, schools attended by white students had more resources, more teachers and better-trained teachers than those attended by non-white students. Since then, all students have been entitled to the same quality of education. However, it takes a long time and a lot of funding to train enough new teachers, build enough new classrooms, provide proper resources to all schools and so rebuild the long-neglected parts of the education system. About one-third of schools still do not have a telephone line – mainly the smallest schools in the most remote areas – but the situation is improving all the time.

Web Search ►►

► http://education.pwv. gov.za
The South Africa government Department of Education.

Sport and Leisure

South Africa's good climate allows sports and games of all sorts to be played outdoors all year round.

During the years when 'apartheid' (apartness) was government policy, many black South Africans were excluded from playing certain sports, especially at national level. The international community protested against this by stopping South Africa from competing at international sports events, including the Olympic Games.

Since the end of apartheid, South Africa has once again competed internationally, often with great success. The 1995 Rugby World Cup was held in South Africa. The famous South African rugby team, called the Springboks, won the championship. South Africa also has one of the world's best cricket teams.

Stick Fighting

One of the oddest traditional sports is stick fighting. This centuries-old 'play-fighting' is done by two people each armed with two sticks. One stick, held in the left hand, is used for parrying (deflecting) the other player's sticks, while the stick held in the right hand is used for thrusting and hitting.

◄◄ At an international cricket match in South Africa, local supporters fly their country's flag in support of their team.

National Parks

The biggest of South Africa's 17 national parks is Kruger National Park in the north-east. It is home to 147 mammal species, 500 bird species and 114 reptile species.

 National Parks

o Pretoria

Bloemfontein o

Cape Town o

Popular Sports

The most popular team sports in South Africa are football, rugby and cricket.

The most popular individual sports are tennis, golf, boxing, swimming and track and field sports.

Canoeing, horse riding, ballooning, caving and mountain biking are becoming increasingly popular.

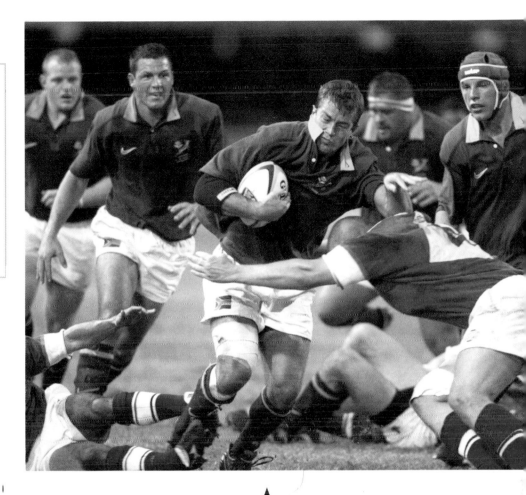

Traditional sports

Modern sports, including rugby, cricket, golf, tennis and athletics, are very popular, but traditional African sports and games are still played, too. The South African Sports Commission (SASC) is keen to support these 'indigenous' sports, including *dibeke*, *kho kho* and *morabaraba*. Dibeke is a ball game. Kho kho is similar to tag – one team chases and tries to touch the other team. Morabaraba is a board game played all over Africa and Asia.

 The Springboks rugby union team play in orange and green sports kit.

Leisure activities

Increased prosperity has enabled more South Africans to enjoy leisure activities. More than a million South Africans take at least one leisure trip every year. Most of them come from the wealthiest provinces of Gauteng and Western Cape. They go camping, visit the beach or take trips into the bush. Going to see films is a very popular leisure activity in South Africa. About 26 million people visit their local cinema every year.

 Web Search ▶▶

▶ http://www.south
africa-travel.net/Parks/
e_parks.htm
A website giving details of the wildlife parks and reserves in South Africa.

▶ http://www.srsa.gov.za
The South Africa government Department of Sport and Recreation.

Daily Life and Religion

Some South Africans spend their daily lives working in modern, air-conditioned city offices. Others, in poorer areas, have more difficult lives.

South Africa's cities are as fast-paced, up-to-date and crowded as anywhere in the world. Most shops are open by 9.00 a.m. and close at 5.00 p.m. Not everyone can afford the fashionable clothes, restaurant meals and consumer goods that the cities have to offer. Rich and poor exist side by side. Crime has become a serious problem in some areas, especially in parts of Johannesburg. Many better-off South Africans live behind high walls and security gates in homes protected by alarms.

Life in rural areas is harsh. There may be only one bus or taxi going into the nearest town each day. An hour or two of each day is taken up with collecting firewood and water. The staple diet is based on a type of porridge cooked over an open fire. Women and girls are more likely to do this, and other housework, than men.

Apartheid

In the 1950s, the South African government introduced apartheid, forbidding black and other non-white South Africans – known as Coloureds – from working, travelling, playing sports and going to school with white people. Mixed marriages were made illegal too. Non-whites were forced to live in townships on the edge of big cities. The government provided the townships with few resources.

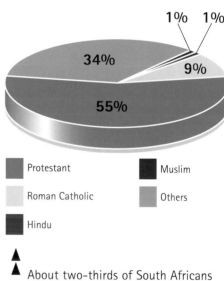

1%   1%

34%

9%

55%

- Protestant
- Roman Catholic
- Hindu
- Muslim
- Others

▲ About two-thirds of South Africans are Christian, mainly Protestant.

◄◄ In both cities and rural areas, many people buy their food at stalls in street markets. The stalls are supplied by local farmers.

22

Health

A number of infectious and parasitic diseases affect parts of South Africa, especially the rural areas where hygiene and healthcare are often poor. The major diseases are malaria, HIV/AIDS and schistosomiasis (also called bilharzia). HIV/AIDS has reached epidemic proportions. As a result, life expectancy in South Africa could fall to only 40 years by 2008.

Religion

Most South Africans are Christian. The conversion of Africans to Christianity gathered pace during a series of wars, called the *Mfecane* (meaning 'crushing'), that occurred in the nineteenth century. The Zulu chief, Shaka, had transformed the Zulus into a fearsome warrior nation. During the tribal wars, many people went to the Christian missionaries for protection. They settled around the mission buildings, attended church services and many of them converted to Christianity.

▲ In rural areas, many houses are built of mud strengthened with wooden beams. This family has painted the mud to make the house look more attractive.

Web Search ►►

► http://www.doh.gov.za
The South Africa government Department of Health.

► http://www.baileyrose.com/tc
A home page for links giving an overview of the townships.

► http://www.cpsa.org.za
The website of the Anglican Church in South Africa.

Arts and Media

The arts and media in South Africa reflect the country's many cultural and historical influences.

For most of the twentieth century, no one was permitted to write about the struggle against white power and apartheid in South Africa. Writers who wanted to deal with political themes had to leave the country to have their books published and their plays performed.

One of the most famous books about life in South Africa is *Cry the Beloved Country*, written by Alan Paton in 1948. In 1983, J.M. Coetzee's book, *Life and Times of Michael K*, won the prestigious British Booker Prize. He became the first writer to win the Booker Prize for a second time when his book, *Disgrace*, won it again in 1999. In 1991, the South African writer, Nadime Gordimer, won the Nobel Prize for literature.

The constitution now guarantees the freedom of the press. Newspapers, magazines and broadcasters may criticise the government if they wish to. The biggest selling newspaper is *The Sowetan*, published in Johannesburg. Newspapers are available in English and Afrikaans.

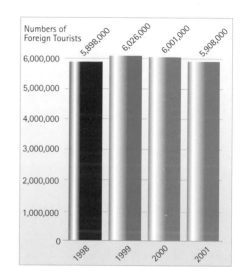

Numbers of Foreign Tourists

1998	1999	2000	2001
5,898,000	6,026,000	6,001,000	5,908,000

▲ The majority of South Africa's tourists are British, closely followed by Germans.

Many cities hold outdoor concerts and plays in the summer months. These are popular with people of all ages. ▼

Music and dance

Music and dance in South Africa are a mixture of African traditions and western influences. Some professional musicians are known only within South Africa. Rebecca Malope is the country's best-selling music star, but she is relatively unknown in other countries.

   Other performers, including the choral group Ladysmith Black Mambazo, and jazz musicians and singers, including Abdullah Ibrahim, Hugh Masakela and Miriam Makeba, have achieved international fame. Western pop, rock, rap and reggae music are popular, too, among young South Africans, and traditional African music and dance are still performed in rural areas.

▲
▲ Zulu dancers dress in traditional warrior uniforms and perform ceremonies to earn money from tourists.

Most South Africans, especially in remote rural areas, receive their news by radio. The South African Broadcasting Company provides national tv broadcasts. There are several satellite tv channels. ▼

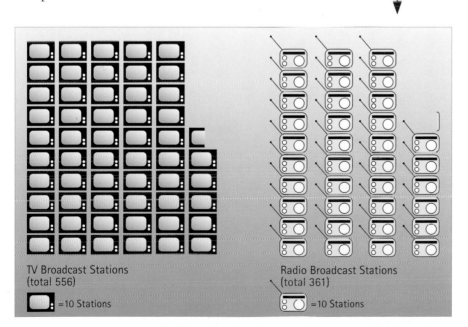

TV Broadcast Stations
(total 556)

☐ = 10 Stations

Radio Broadcast Stations
(total 361)

 = 10 Stations

DATABASE

Popular attractions

Table Mountain, for scenery
Robben Island, where Nelson Mandela was imprisoned
The Cape of Good Hope, for scenery and wildlife
The wine estates of Paarl, Stellenbosch and Franschoek
The scenic 'Garden Route' from Swellendam to Humansdorp
The Kruger National Park, for wildlife

 Web Search ►►

► http://www.suntimes.co.za
The Sunday Times *newspaper of South Africa, with national and world news.*

Government

South African politics underwent great change during the 1990s. For the first time, all people were given the right to vote. The choices made by ordinary people all over the country completely changed the government and brought Nelson Mandela to power as president.

South Africa's parliament consists of the National Assembly and the National Council of Provinces (NCOP). The National Assembly has 350 to 400 members elected for five years by popular vote. The president is elected by the National Assembly. The NCOP has 54 permanent members and 36 special delegates, who represent provincial interests at the national level. In addition, each of the nine provinces has its own local government of between 30 and 80 members led by a premier. The president holds regular meetings with the premiers of the provinces to discuss local and national issues.

Within the provinces, there are about 284 councils. Councils in poor areas find it difficult to raise money locally for projects, so support is provided by the national and provincial governments. This has enabled millions of people in poor and rural areas to be given basic services, such as clean water and sanitation, for the first time.

Nelson Mandela

Nelson Mandela is one of the world's most highly respected politicians. After gaining a law degree, he joined the African National Congress (ANC) to work for black freedom. When police officers killed unarmed Africans at a demonstration in Sharpeville in 1960, he supported violence against the government and was sentenced to life imprisonment in 1964.

Nelson Mandela was released in 1990 and shared the Nobel Peace Prize in 1993 with President F.W. de Klerk for their work to bring about a peaceful end to apartheid. When the first all-race elections were held in 1994, Mandela was elected president. He retired from politics in 1999.

Soon after his release from prison, Nelson Mandela (centre right) met with Archbishop Desmond Tutu (centre left) and other South African religious leaders who had helped persuade President de Klerk's government to bring an end to apartheid. ►►

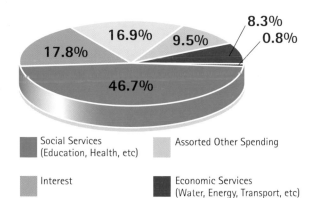

16.9%   8.3%
17.8%   9.5%   0.8%
46.7%

- ■ Social Services (Education, Health, etc)
- ■ Interest
- ■ Protective services (Defence, Police, etc)
- ■ Assorted Other Spending
- ■ Economic Services (Water, Energy, Transport, etc)
- ■ Reserve

◄◄ Almost half of government spending is on social services yet many parts of the country lack good-quality schools, hospitals and transport systems.

The Houses of Parliament in Cape Town where the South African government regularly meets. ▼
▼

Government

South Africa is divided into nine administrative regions, or provinces. There are three capital cities: Cape Town, Bloemfontein and Pretoria.

Web Search ▶▶

▶ http://www.gov.za
Website of the South African government.

▶ http://www.anc.org.za
Website of the African National Congress (ANC).

▶ http://www.southafrica house.com
Website of the South African High Commission in London.

Chronology of Historical Events – up to the 1930s

1400s Bartholomeu Dias is the first European explorer to visit the southern tip of Africa.

1652 The Dutch build a shipping station on the Cape of Good Hope.

1657 A group of Dutch workers are released from their contracts and become farmers, or Boers.

1658 The Dutch commander, Jan van Riebeeck, brings a ship full of slaves from West Africa to work at the Cape.

1660s The local Khoikhoi tribesmen fight the Dutch settlers.

1795 British troops occupy the Cape of Good Hope.

1834 Slavery is abolished.

1835 12,000 Boers make the Great Trek inland to escape British rule and stay separate from black Africans.

1852 Britain grants independence to settlers in the Transvaal.

1852 Britain grants independence to settlers in the Orange Free State.

1867 Diamonds are discovered.

1883 Paul Kruger becomes President of the South African Republic in the Transvaal.

1886 Gold is discovered.

1899–1902 The South African (Boer) War ends in victory for Britain.

1910 Britain brings the Boer republics and British colonies together as the Union of South Africa.

Place in the World

People have lived in South Africa since the very first humans walked the Earth, but modern South Africa is one of the world's youngest democracies, still dealing with the effects of its troubled past.

South Africa achieved its independence from Britain in 1910. It became a member of the British Commonwealth, which is a group of independent countries that were once British colonies. In 1961, South Africa was expelled from the Commonwealth. It was shunned by the rest of the world, too, because of its policy of apartheid that denied equal rights to non-white people. The end of apartheid and the election of an all-race government in 1994 ended South Africa's isolation and brought it back into the community of nations.

Soweto – short for South Western Township (of Johannesburg) – was a focus for protests by black South Africans that helped to bring an end to white rule. ▼

A world-player

Today, South Africa plays a full and active role in many international organizations, including the African, Caribbean and Pacific Group of States (ACP), the International Olympic Committee (IOC), the United Nations (UN), UNESCO (the United Nations Educational, Scientific and Cultural Organization) and the World Health Organization (WHO).

International disputes

In general, South Africa has very good relations with other countries. However, its acceptance of the harsh government of neighbouring Zimbabwe is unpopular, and it is in dispute with Swaziland over their common border. When Swaziland was created in 1903 and the border drawn between it and South Africa, the areas where some Swazi people lived were taken into South Africa. They became part of Kwazulu-Natal. Since Swaziland achieved its independence from Britain in 1968, it has pressured South Africa to return the Swazi-occupied areas.

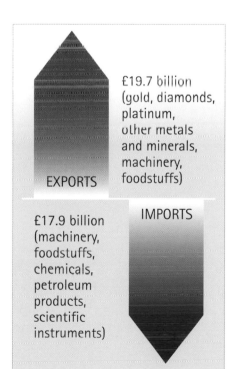

£19.7 billion (gold, diamonds, platinum, other metals and minerals, machinery, foodstuffs)
EXPORTS

£17.9 billion (machinery, foodstuffs, chemicals, petroleum products, scientific instruments)
IMPORTS

◀◀ South Africa's imports and exports.

Web Search ▶▶

▶ http://www.dti.gov.za
The South Africa government Department of Trade and Industry.

▶ http://www.economist. com
The Economist profile of South Africa.

▶ http://news.bbc.co.uk/1/ hi/world/africa/country_ profiles/1071886.stm
A profile of South Africa from the BBC.

DATABASE

Chronology of Historical Events – from the 1930s

1930s The Land Acts set aside most of the land for white people.

1948 The National Party wins the election and holds power until 1994.

1950 The Group Areas Act forces different races to live in different places.

1959 Ten African homelands are created.

1960 Police fire on a demonstration against apartheid laws at Sharpeville, killing 67 and wounding nearly 200.

1967 Dr Christiaan Barnard performs the world's first human heart transplant operation in Cape Town.

1976 Riots break out in Soweto in protest against school lessons being taught in Afrikaans.

1977 Black activist Steve Biko is killed by police officers.

1980s Many countries sever their links with South Africa because of its apartheid policy.

1990 The government begins to repeal the apartheid laws, 'un-bans' the ANC and releases Mandela from prison.

1994 The first all-race elections. Nelson Mandela becomes the first black President.

1996 The Truth and Reconciliation Commission is set up to examine human rights abuses.

1999 Nelson Mandela steps down and Thabo Mbeki becomes President.

Area:
1,219,912 sq km
including Prince Edward Islands
(Marion Island and Prince Edward
Island)

Population size:
44,202,000

Capital city:
Pretoria (executive capital)
(Population 1,200,000)
Cape Town (legislative capital)
(Population 3,000,000)
Bloemfontein (judicial capital)
(Population 450,000)

Other major cities and townships:
Johannesburg (pop. 4,000,000)
Durban (pop. 3,700,000)
Soweto (pop. approx. 3,500,000)
Pietermaritzburg (pop. 300,000)
Kimberley (pop. 211,000)
Stellenbosch (pop. 60,000)

Flag:
The Republic of South Africa
adopted a multicoloured flag in
1994. A green Y with white border
lies on its side, with a red band
above, blue band below and a
black triangle, edged with yellow
(gold) inside the 'arms'. Green, gold
and black represent the colours of
the ANC, South Africa's biggest
political party.

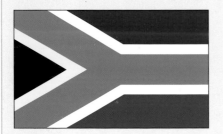

Longest rivers:
Orange River, including its Vaal
tributary (2,090 km)

Highest mountain:
Injasuti (also called Njesuthi) in the
   Drakensburg range (3,446m)
Toorberg (2,280m)
Bamboesberge (2,207m)
Table Mountain (1,085m)

Currency:
South African Rand
1 rand = 100 cents
£1 = 11.5 rand

Languages:
11 official languages – Afrikaans,
English, Ndebele, Pedi, Sotho, Swazi,
Tsonga, Tswana, Venda, Xhosa, Zulu.

Major resources:
gold, chromium, antimony, coal,
iron ore, manganese, nickel,
phosphates, tin, uranium, gem
diamonds, platinum, copper,
vanadium, salt, natural gas.

Major exports:
Gold, diamonds, coal, platinum,
machinery and equipment.

**National holidays and major
events:**
January 1: New Year's Day
March 21: Human Rights Day
April 27: Constitution Day
May 1: Workers' Day
June 16: Youth Day
August 9: National Women's Day
September 24: Heritage Day
December 16: Day of
   Reconciliation
December 25: Christmas Day
December 26: Day of Good Will

Religions:
Most South Africans are
Christian, mainly Protestant.
Other religions practised are
Catholicism, Hinduism and Islam.

Glossary

AGRICULTURE
Farming the land, including ploughing, planting, raising crops, and raising animals.

APARTHEID ('APARTNESS')
The policy of keeping different races separate that was practised in South Africa until the early 1990s.

ALTITUDE
The height of a mountain or an area of land above sea level.

BUSH
An area of wilderness covered with trees or shrubs, where few people live.

CLIMATE
The long-term weather in an area.

CONTINENT
One of the Earth's largest land masses – Europe, Asia, Australia, North and South America, Africa and Antarctica.

CULTURE
The beliefs, ideas, knowledge and customs of a group of people, or the group of people themselves.

ECONOMY
A country's finances.

EXPORTS
Products, resources or goods sold to other countries.

GOVERNMENT
A group of people who manage a country, deciding on laws, raising taxes and organizing health, education, transport and other national systems and services.

GROSS DOMESTIC PRODUCT
The value of all goods and services produced by a nation in a year.

IMPORTS
Products, resources or goods brought into the country.

IRRIGATION
Artificial watering of the land by building dams and canals, laying water pipes and using wells and pumps.

LITERACY
The ability to read and write.

LITERACY RATE
The percentage of the population who can read and write.

MANUFACTURING
Making large numbers of the same things by hand or, more commonly, by machine.

POPULATION
All the people who live in a city, country, region or other area.

POPULATION DENSITY
The average number of people living in each square kilometre of a city, country, region or other area.

RESOURCES
Materials that can be used to make goods or electricity, or to generate income for a country or region.

RACE
A group of people who have the same ancestry and are often different from others because of physical features such as skin colour, facial appearance, build, height or type of hair.

RURAL
Having the qualities of the countryside, with a low population density.

URBAN
Having the qualities of a city, with a high population density.

In country areas of Kwazulu-Natal province, many Zulus live in grass huts and wear traditional clothes. ▼

Index